THE JEWISH SPIRIT

THE HERITAGE OF JUDAISM
IN SELECTED WRITINGS

Edited by Tina Hacker

Hallmark Editions

The publisher wishes to thank those who have given their kind permission to reprint material included in this book. Every effort has been made to give proper acknowledgments. Any omissions or errors are deeply regretted, and the publisher, upon notification, will be pleased to make necessary corrections in subsequent editions.

ACKNOWLEDGMENTS: "The Ladder of Tzedakah" adapted from Maimonides's Mishneh Torah from Tzedakah: A Way of Life, edited by Azriel Eisenberg. Reprinted by permission of the publisher, Behrman House, Inc. "God" from The Ethics of Israel by Israel H. Weisfeld. Copyright ©1948 by Israel H. Weisfeld. Published by Bloch Publishing Company. "Family Love" from Glimpses Into Life by Rabbi Louis Grossmann. Published 1922 by Bloch Publishing Company. Both reprinted by courtesy of Bloch Publishing Company. "Weeds" and "Not Blind Chance" from The Gifts of Life and Love by Ben Zion Bokser. ©1975 by Ben Zion Bokser. Reprinted by permission of the author. "Man and Wife" by Shin Shalom from An Anthology of Modern Hebrew Poetry, edited by Abraham Birman. Copyright ©1968 by Abraham Birman. Reprinted by permission of Abelard-Schuman. "From Tomorrow On" by an unknown child and "God Everywhere" by Abraham Ibn Ezra taken from A Treasury of Jewish Poetry, edited by Nathan and Marynn Ausubel. ©1957 by Nathan and Marynn Ausubel. Used by permission of Crown Publishers, Inc. "What Brotherhood Requires" taken from May I Have a Word With You? by Rabbi Morris Adler. Compiled by Goldie Adler and Lily Edelman. ©1967 by B'nai B'rith. Used by permission of Crown Publishers, Inc. "Jewish Tradition" taken from Ideas and Opinions by Albert Einstein. ©1954 by Crown Publishers, Inc. Used by permission of Crown Publishers, Inc. "Ghetto Chassid" by Paul Barlin reprinted by permission from the Winter 1975 issue of Davka. ©1975 Davka. "Honor and Conscience" from Collected Works of Anne Frank by Otto H. Frank. Copyright ©1959 by Otto H. Frank. Reprinted by permission of the publisher, Doubleday & Company, Inc. and Otto H. Frank. "A Living Power" by Aaron Zeitlin, translated by Robert Friend from A Treasury of Yiddish Poetry, edited by Irving Howe and Eliezer Greenberg. Copyright ©1969 by Irving Howe and Eliezer Greenberg. Reprinted by permission of Holt, Rinehart and Winston, Publishers. "A Living Power" by Bernard J. Bamberger reprinted with permission of Macmillan Publishing Co., Inc. from The Condition of Jewish Belief, compiled by the Editors of Commentary Magazine. Copyright ©1966 by The American Jewish Committee. Originally published in Commentary Magazine. "Taking a Stand" from the book The Way I See It by Eddie Cantor. ©1959 by Eddie Cantor. Published by Prentice-Hall, Inc., Englewood Cliffs, New Jersey. Reprinted with permission. "The Minority Viewpoint" reprinted by permission of Schocken Books Inc. from The Essence of Judaism by Leo Baeck. Copyright ©1948 by Schocken Books Inc. "The Herdsman Who Could Not Pray" by Judah he-Hasid reprinted by permission of Schocken Books Inc. from A Jewish Reader, edited by Nahum N. Glatzer. Copyright ©1946, 1961 by Schocken Books Inc. "A Divine Quest" by William B. Silverman. Reprinted by permission of the author. "Eve" from Blessed Is the Daughter by Meyer Waxman. ©1959 by Shengold Publishers, Inc. Reprinted by permission of Shengold Publishers, Inc. "God Our Friend" from Peace of Mind by Joshua Loth Liebman. Copyright ©1946 by Joshua Loth Liebman. Reprinted by permission of the publishers, Simon & Schuster, Inc. and William Heinemann Ltd. "Human Values" by David Ben Gurion from Ben Gurion Looks Back by Moshe Pearlman and David Ben Gurion. Copyright © 1965 by Moshe Pearlman and David Ben Gurion. Reprinted by permission of the publishers, Simon & Schuster, Inc. and George Weidenfeld & Nicholson Ltd. "The Fate of the World" from Everything but Money by Sam Levenson. Copyright ©1949, 1951, 1952, 1953, 1955, 1956, 1958, 1959, 1961, 1966 by Sam Levenson. Reprinted by permission of the publisher, Simon & Schuster, Inc. "Literature" by Paul Goodman reprinted from 3,000 Years of Hebrew History. ©1972 by Nathaniel Kravitz. Reprinted with permission of The Swallow Press, Inc. "Birth" by Amir Gilboa from Modern Hebrew Poetry, edited and translated by Ruth Finer Mintz. Copyright ©1966 by The Regents of the University of California. Reprinted by permission of the University of California Press. "Prayer" from This Is My God by Herman Wouk. Copyright ©1959 by The Abe Wouk Foundation, Inc. Reprinted by permission of Harold Matson Company, Inc.

THE JEWISH SPIRIT

Children celebrating Rosh Hashana.

A PEOPLE OF THE HEART

To the Jew, love is not just a word; it is a way of life. From earliest childhood, we are taught to treat our family, friends, neighbors, indeed all humanity, with kindness, concern, compassion and charity. How fitting, then, to begin a collection of Jewish thoughts with a chapter on love.

FAMILY LOVE
Rabbi Louis Grossmann

Many splendid things are told of Moses, the leader of Israel, but none that does him more credit or, rather, that reports his genuine nature better than the fact that, though Prince of the Royal House of Egypt, he sought day after day to be amongst the humiliated Israelites who toiled in the clayfields and in the brick-kilns. He felt nearer to them than to the great in the palace, for they were his own.

THE LADDER OF TZEDAKAH
Adapted from Maimonides's Mishneh Torah

Tzedakah is a basic ideal in Judaism. More than charity, it encompasses justice, mercy, service, loving-kindness and concern for others. Following is Maimonides's "Eight Degrees of Tzedakah." Here are eight steps, from low to high, from worst to best. It is up to the individual to decide which step to attain.

1. The lowest step in giving *Tzedakah* is to give too little, and as if "forced" to give.
2. The next step is, though giving too little, to do so ... cheerfully, as if happy to give.
3. The third step is to give as much as is needed, but only after being asked for it.
4. The fourth step is to give as much as is needed and to do so *before* being asked for it.
5. A fifth and higher step than all these is to give enough and to give before being asked, and to give in such a way that the poor person knows who gives him help, but the helper does not know who the poor person is.
6. Sixth on the "Ladder of *Tzedakah*" is to give enough and before being asked, but in such a way that the giver knows who gets the charity, but the receiver doesn't know who has given it to him.

7. The seventh and the next to the highest way to give *Tzedakah* is to do it so that neither the giver nor the receiver knows the other.
8. Finally, at the very top of the "*Tzedakah* Ladder" is the step of helping a needy person by lending him money to open a business or joining him in a partnership or finding him a job, so that he can support himself and not *need* charity.

Love is sweet, but tastes best with bread.

Yiddish Proverb

Charity is equal to all the other commandments.

The Talmud

Marriage Contract, *Collection, The Jewish Museum, New York.*

MAN AND WIFE
Shin Shalom

I wed you not with overwhelming lyre,
You won me by assurance deep and calm.
Our love-song was enhanced by wisdom's psalm,
You gave me all the light and hid the fire.

My soul was snugly sheltered in your palm
From straying wild, from deviation's briar;
And when despair would tempt me to retire,
Your tact and taste endowed me with their balm.

How good to lean my head against your breast,
The warp of sorrow and the woof of joy
To weave around your heart in peace and rest.

With me you are — who will my lot destroy?
With you I am — sleep on, beloved name.
I guard your altar, keep the sacred flame.

IN THE OLD GHETTO
D. Philipson, 1894

In the narrow lanes and by-ways of the old Jewish quarter of many a European town there grew up that beautiful Jewish home-life which, though its story is seldom recorded, is more important than the outer events and misfortunes that historians have made note of. And as we look upon the unsightly houses, the wretched exterior seems to float away and the home-scenes of joy and love and religious constancy shine brilliantly forth — perpetual lamps — and explain how, in spite of woe and misery such as have fallen to the lot of no other people, the Jews have found strength to live and hope on.

BIRTH
Amir Gilboa

The rain has passed.

And yet from roofs and trees
It sings in my ears
And covers my head
With a bluish bridal-veil.

Good for you, my God,
In your net the child has been caught.
Now I shall bring leaf close to leaf
Watch how leaf covers leaf
And the drops join,
Then I will call the swallows
To betrothal from my sky.
And crown my windows with flower pots.

Good for you, my God,
In your net the child has been caught.
I open my eyes —
My earth is very wide
And all a beaten work
Of knobby buds,
Green.

Oh, my God, how embraced we have been.

LOVING TREES
Jewish Folk Saying

If you're planting a tree and you hear the Messiah
has come, first finish planting and then run to the
city gates to tell him Shalom.

WHAT BROTHERHOOD REQUIRES
Rabbi Morris Adler

The Bible serves not only as a great bridge between
man and God, but also between man and his
brother. For true religion casts its eyes not only
heavenward but also upon the human scene. He
who has no eyes for his fellowman cannot hope
to glimpse God or His providence. For religion
ever seeks to link man and man in a common
family, the expression of our unity as the children of One God. One world is the inescapable
corollary of One God. Man is related to his neighbor not by the accident of birth, nor by the proxi-
mity of dwelling, nor by a shared danger, nor by
an identity of citizenship or color. Man is more
than fellow citizen, coreligionist, classmate, part-
ner, neighbor. He is brother.

WEEDS
Ben Zion Bokser

A farmer once sighed after he had finished weeding his garden. His back was bent, the perspiration ran down his face. "If not for those cursed weeds," he said to himself, "gardening would be such a joy. Why God made weeds is really beyond me."

The farmer mused a little as he contemplated the heap of weeds he had pulled out. Suddenly one of the weeds spoke up. Its face was already pale and wilting, but it mustered enough strength to speak in self-defense.

"You should not speak ill of any of God's creatures," the little weed said. "You have given us a bad name and decried our presence in the world. We render you a thousand uses you may not be aware of. We tend your soil when you are not there to cultivate it. We prevent your precious earth from being washed away by the rain. We do not allow it be carried away by the wind as dust. And do we not justify our existence even in your carefully cultivated garden? Your flowers would never be able to stand the elements... if we did not toughen them. In their skirmishes with us they gain strength. When you enjoy their splendor, remember that we had a part in their growth."

The weed made a marked impression, and then although almost exhausted it continued in a per-oration: "The vegetation you cultivate is like the people in your own world. They need some op-position to be toughened for the formidable busi-ness of living."

The weed resumed its silence. The farmer straightened his back as he wiped his brow. A smile of satisfaction came over his face. He looked out on the field that was yet to be weeded, but he knew that weeding would no longer be a dis-agreeable task.

Israel is the heart of mankind.
Yehudah Halevi, 1141

PEOPLE OF GOD

If there is one tenant in Judaism that unites all genera-
tions, it is the belief in one God — a God of truth, love
and justice. "Hear, O Israel: the Lord our God, the Lord
is One," we chant over and over again — in the syna-
gogue, in our homes, on holidays and all days. Every
Jew the world over knows this prayer. In saying it, we
are bound to each other and to our God forever.

PRAYER
Herman Wouk

Perhaps for saints and for truly holy men fully
conscious prayer is really an everyday thing....
For the ordinary worshipper, the rewards of a
lifetime of faithful praying comes at unpredict-
able times, scattered through the years, when all
at once the liturgy glows as with fire. Such an
hour may come after a death, or after a birth;...
it may flood the soul at no marked time, for no
marked reason. It comes, and he knows why he
has prayed all his life.

GOD EVERYWHERE
Abraham Ibn Ezra
Spain, 1092-1167

Wheresoe'er I turn mine eyes
Around on Earth or toward the skies,
I see Thee in the starry field,
I see Thee in the harvest's yield,
In every breath, in every sound,
An echo of Thy name is found.
The blade of grass, the simple flower,
Bear witness to Thy matchless pow'r.
My every thought, Eternal God of Heaven,
Ascends to Thee, to whom all praise be given.

HONOR AND CONSCIENCE
Anne Frank

People who have a religion should be glad, for not everyone has the gift of believing in heavenly things. You don't necessarily even have to be afraid of punishment after death; hell and heaven are things that a lot of people can't accept, but still a religion, it doesn't matter which, keeps a person on the right path. It isn't the fear of God but the upholding of one's own honor and conscience.

GOD OUR FRIEND
Joshua Loth Liebman

In this vast universe
There is but one supreme truth —
That God is our friend!
By that truth meaning is given
To the remote stars, the numberless centuries,
The long and heroic struggle of mankind...
O my Soul, dare to trust this truth!
Dare to rest in God's kindly arms,
Dare to look confidently into His face,
Then launch thyself into life unafraid!
Knowing thou art within thy Father's house,
That thou art surrounded by His love,
Thou wilt become master of fear,
Lord of life, conqueror even of death!

The Western Wall and the Dome of the Rock, Jerusalem.

GOD

To the Jew, God is not a cold, impersonal all-powerful Being whose sole concern is that the laws of nature shall continue in undisturbed fashion; rather, He is a warm, compassionate Being, interested in each human being as is a human father in each of his children. And, truly, like trusting children, we look to our Eternal Father for guidance, authority, love, mercy and forgiveness; and, by emulating Him in our relations with our fellowman, strive to attain the highest possible form of human development — that of becoming *Godlike.*

THE MATTER OF DESIGN
The Midrash

Rabbi Akiva said: as a house implies
a builder, and a garment a weaver,
and a door a carpenter, so does the
existence of the world imply a creator.

A DIVINE QUEST
Rabbi William B. Silverman

We are committed to a divine quest.
We are summoned to go forth in search of divinity,
a divinity we will never completely understand,
a divinity we will never completely find.
But the quest itself will sanctify our lives with
    holiness,
elevate our vision to the Most High,
and turn us —
our thoughts,
our aspirations,
our future —
beyond the edge of mystery,
in the direction of God.

A LIVING POWER
Bernard J. Bamberger

I believe that man's strivings, above all his ethical
strivings, are not irrelevant to the universe. I
believe man has some kinship with ultimate
reality. Or, in more traditional language — though
no language is adequate — I believe in God as a
living power.

NOT BLIND CHANCE
Ben Zion Bokser

Winter in its forbidding austerity is coming upon our world. Soon the paralysis of cold will strike. Soon nature will cover its growing glory with a mask of snow. I can see the birds in their migrations southward, seeking the comforts of a warmer home.

Who taught the birds to follow the journey south? Who mapped out their itinerary? Who gave them the spirit of adventure to follow the promise of a better life, and who gives them the wisdom to find their way back again when the winter is ended and a warm sun shines on our world once more?

When I contemplate the wonder of the birds I know that Thou, O Lord, dost guide it all. Not blind chance but a plan of infinite wisdom governs the life of the universe.

I AM THE SYNAGOGUE

I am the Synagogue.

I am the heart of Jewry. I have sheltered you for more than two thousand five hundred years. Through all these cruel ages, swept by wrath of fire and sword, I nursed you with the word of God, healed your wounds with the balm of faith, steadied your minds and hearts with the vision of the Eternal.

When your fathers wept by the waters of Babylon, I came into the world, summoned by their need. In Persia, Greece and in Rome, in the face of the howling crusaders and in the clutches of the Black Inquisition, in the pogroms of Poland and in the Concentration Camps of the Nazis, I have been, and by my presence brought the living waters of the Eternal to the parched lips of your fathers.

When the world derided them, I restored them. When men cursed them, I blessed them.

I bring you peace by teaching you duty. I sanctify your lives with holy seasons. I preserve your heritage. I make the faith of the father the faith of the children. Behold, a good doctrine do I give unto you; forsake it not.

Opposite page:
Synagogue of Isaac Luria at Safed.   25

THE HERDSMAN WHO COULD NOT PRAY
Judah he-Hasid
Germany, 12th-13th Century

There was a certain man who was a herdsman, and he did not know how to pray. But it was his custom to say every day: "Lord of the world! It is apparent and known unto you, that if you had cattle and gave them to me to tend, though I take wages for tending from all others, from you I would take nothing, because I love you."

Once a learned man was going his way and came upon the herdsman, who was praying thus. He said to him: "Fool, do not pray thus."

The herdsman asked him: "How should I pray?"

Thereupon, the learned man taught him the benedictions in order, the recitation of the Shema and the prayer, so that, henceforth, he would not say what he was accustomed to say.

After the learned man had gone away, the herdsman forgot all that had been taught him and did not pray. And he was even afraid to say what he had been accustomed to say, since the righteous man had told him not to.

But the learned man had a dream by night, and in it he heard a voice saying: "If you do not tell him to say what he was accustomed to say before you came to him, know that misfortune will overtake you, for you have robbed me of one who be-longs to the world to come."

At once the learned man went to the herdsman and said to him: "What prayer are you making?"

The herdsman answered: "None, for I have for-gotten what you taught me, and you forbade me to say: 'If you had cattle.'"

Then the learned man told him what he had dreamed, and added: "Say what you used to say."

Behold, here there is neither Torah nor works, but only this, that there was one who had it in his heart to do good, and he was rewarded for it, as if this were a great thing. For "the Merciful One desires the heart." Therefore, let men think good thoughts, and let these thoughts be turned to the Holy One, blessed be he.

He has his life from God and his living from man.
Yiddish Proverb

BUILDERS OF CIVILIZATION

Wherever Jewish people have lived, they have contrib-
uted to the welfare of the community in just about
every area: from science to education to furthering the
ideals of democracy. We are a people who look back —
to our history, our teachings, our beliefs. But we are
also a people who look forward. Our heritage gives us
strength and vision. It is the rock upon which we build.

LITERATURE
Paul Goodman

The history of the Jews presents the struggles for light and life of a people small in numbers and negligible in political power but great in achievement and unparalleled in endurance. This people, whom the historians and geographers of ancient Hellas hardly deigned to notice as a strange Syrian tribe, had already then produced one of the most remarkable literatures of all time as well as a body of men who were later on acclaimed as the ethical and religious teachers of mankind.

Opposite page:
The holy city of Jerusalem.

THE MINORITY VIEWPOINT
Leo Baeck

It would often appear that it is one of the tasks of Judaism to give expression in the history of the world to the idea of standing alone, *the ethical principle of the minority.* Judaism bears witness to the power of the idea as against the power of mere numbers and of outward success; it stands for the enduring protest of those who seek to be true to their own selves, of those who claim to be different, as against the crushing pressure of those who want all to think alike. This attitude is itself a constant message to the peoples of the world.

ISRAEL'S CONCEPTION OF JUSTICE
Maurice H. Farbridge

A distinguished American judge, referring to the Jewish contributions to civilization, says: "Israel's idea of justice has taken permanent possession of the human mind. Torn asunder by faction, driven from his country, scattered to the four winds of heaven, scourged up and down the highways of the world, stretched upon the rack, burned at the stake, massacred by the hundred thousand, a wanderer, friendless and homeless through the centuries, despised by the world he was liberating from its idols, Israel has stamped his ideal of justice on the human consciousness itself, and lives in every upward movement of the race. I do not forget what other races have contributed to the common store — Athens and Italy their sense of beauty, Sparta and Rome their love of discipline and order, Gaul and Germany their zeal for liberty, England and America their ever-blessed union of liberty under law. I do not forget what your gifted race has wrought in other ways — in war and statecraft, in music, art, poetry, science, history, philosophy — but, compared with the meaning and majesty of this achievement, every other work you have accomplished, every other triumph of every other people, sinks into insignificance. Give up every other claim to the world's gratitude before you surrender this: the world owes its conception of justice to the Jew."

The Jewish spirit in dance and song.

FROM TOMORROW ON
Written by an unknown child in a Nazi death camp

From tomorrow on I shall be sad,
From tomorrow on.
Not today. Today I will be glad.
And every day, no matter how bitter
   it may be,
I shall say:
From tomorrow on I shall be sad,
Not today.

MEANING OF SALVATION
Anonymous

To the Jew salvation means redeeming the world from evil. And that can come only through the constant disciplining and refining of the individual, so that he can discern right from wrong and not only discern it but learn to enjoy the good and reject the evil. This is the definition of ancient Hebrew wisdom. To this ultimate end has Jewish learning been directed. This is the message of Israel to mankind.

STUDY AND ACTION
The Talmud

Rabbi Tarphon and the Elders were together
    at Lud and a question was asked of them:
which is more important, study or action?

    Rabbi Tarphon said action was more
important; Rabbi Akiva said that study was
    more important. At length they all agreed:
that form of study is good that leads to action.

TAKING A STAND
Eddie Cantor

I have opinions — on everything from politics to
passion. And I'm about to stick my neck out. Call
me anything you like, but you'll never call me
"neutral."

To me, neutrality's a crime. A sin against your-
self and your society. Know what "neuter" is?
Something sterile. Impotent. Incapable of making
life. You can't stay neutral and make much of *any*
life. A person has to pick his side and fight for it.
On every issue. I think it's better to be in the
wrong than never in the running.

HUMAN VALUES
David Ben Gurion

It is 2,500 years since the age of the prophets. We now live in another world. Our generation and those who come after us will mould their lives in conditions of which the ancients never dreamed. But *human values* have not changed. The values of truth and righteousness, mercy and peace, and the love of fellowman continue to be upheld, at least as ideals. The old worlds may have gone; but the contribution of their spiritual giants has left an ineffaceable imprint on all who have come later and, whether we are aware of it or not, we are nourished by it.

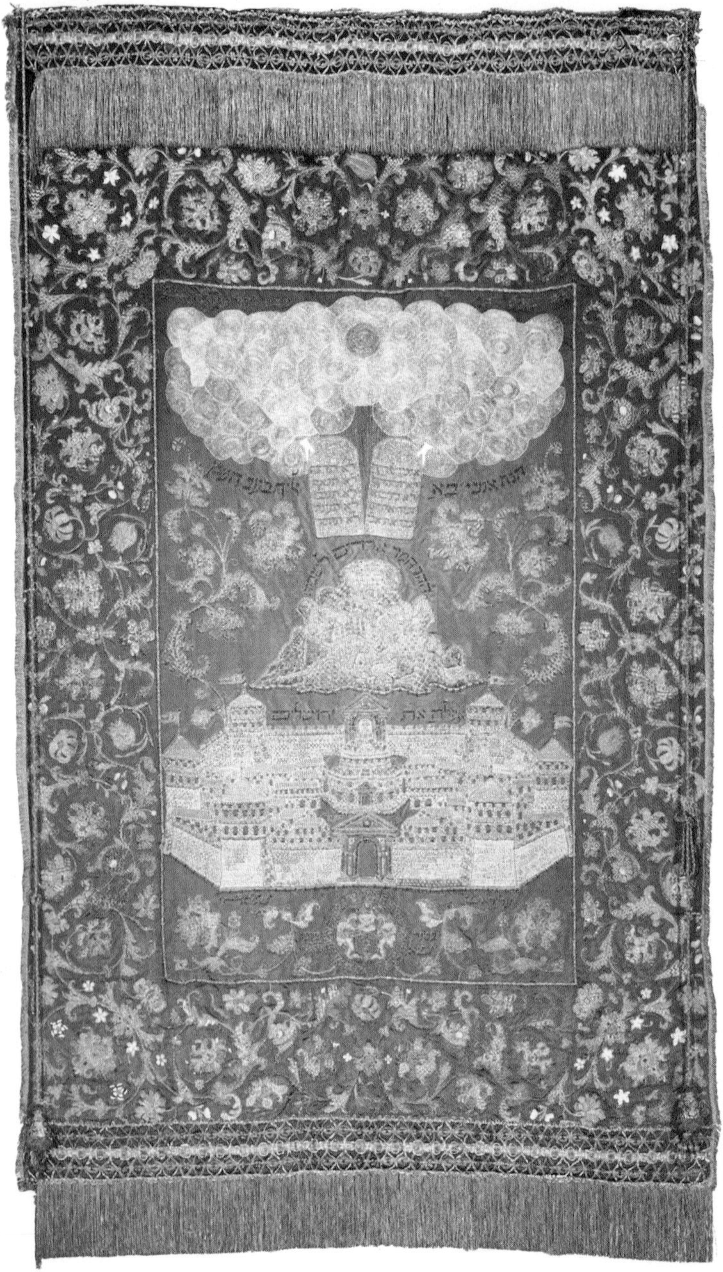

AN ETERNAL PEOPLE

L'chayim! *To life! Jews share this toast all over the world. It is symbolic of the Jewish spirit. We will live and survive against all odds. And we will live with joy on our lips and hope in our hearts. Such has been the way of our ancestors for five thousand years. What a beautiful path we have to follow!*

JERUSALEM
David Ben Levi

City of glory, of immortal kings,
My heart ever yearns for you.
The spirit of my people
Dwells within your walls.
Your stones have seen our golden victories
And heard our bitter cries.
Still, you hold a silent vigil —
Watching, listening
For the Messiah's footsteps
To approach your gates.

Opposite page:
Torah Ark Curtain, *Collection,*
The Jewish Museum, New York.   37

THE ETERNAL RIDDLE
P. M. Raskin, 1914

Israel, my people,
God's greatest riddle,
Will thy solution
Ever be told?
Fought — never conquered,
Bent — never broken,
Mortal — immortal,
Youthful, though old.
Egypt enslaved thee,
Babylon crushed thee,
Rome led thee captive,
Homeless thy head.
Where are those nations
Mighty and fearsome?
Thou hast survived them,
They are long dead.
Nations keep coming,
Nations keep going,
Passing like shadows,
Wiped off the earth.
Thou an eternal
Witness remainest,
Watching their burial,
Watching their birth.
Pray, who revealed thee

Heaven's great secret:
Death and destruction
Thus to defy?
Suffering torture,
Stake, inquisition —
Prithee, who taught thee
Never to die?
Aye, and who gave thee
Faith, deep as ocean,
Strong as the rock-hills,
Fierce as the sun?
Hated and hunted,
Ever thou wand'rest,
Bearing a message:
God is but one!
Pray, has thy saga
Likewise an ending
As its beginning
Glorious of old?
Israel, my people,
God's greatest riddle,
Will thy solution
Ever be told?

Praying at the Western Wall.

GHETTO CHASSID
Paul Barlin

Reach to the sun, Jew
stretch your wrinkled skin
let the sweet air
touch your body
where the sorrowed creases are

Turn, Jew
and let the sky
see you as a living
work of art

Jump, Jew
leave the earth for an instant
and feel the heavens
under your feet

every breath you expel
let it be a note of music
biri-BOM
sing as you dance
and you will hear
your soul again

whirl like the wind
set your blood racing
feel alive
in God's vibrant world!

THE FATE OF THE WORLD
Sam Levenson

I should like to revert to an ancient tradition of my people which required a father to leave to his children, in addition to some earthly goods, an ethical will, the purpose of which was to transmit a summation of personal values, some articles of faith which the child, while not morally bound to accept, is urged to consider.

I believe that each newborn child arrives on earth with a message to deliver to mankind. Clenched in his little fist is some particle of yet unrevealed truth, some missing clue, which may solve the enigma of man's destiny. He has a limited amount of time to fulfill his mission and he will never get a second chance — nor will we. He may be our last hope. He must be treated as top sacred.

In a cosmos in which all things appear to have a meaning, what is *his* meaning? We who are older and presumably wiser must find the key to unlock the secret he carries within himself. The lock cannot be forced. Our mission is to exercise the kind of loving care which will prompt the child to open his fist and offer up his truth, his individuality, the irreducible atom of his self. We must provide the kind of environment in which the child will joyfully deliver his message through complete self-fulfillment....

There are many political and social movements whose earnest purpose is to save the world. My personal commitment is to the philosophy expressed in Sanhedrin 4:5 which says that whoever destroys one life will be considered as having destroyed the whole world; and whoever saves one life will be credited with having saved the whole world.

BEING A JEW
Aaron Zeitlin

Being a Jew means running forever to God
Even if you are His betrayer,
Means expecting to hear any day,
Even if you are a nay sayer,
The blare of Messiah's horn;

Means, even if you wish to,
You cannot escape His snares,
You cannot cease to pray —
Even after all the prayers,
Even after all the "evens."

A face of courage at the top of Massada.

EVE
Meyer Waxman

According to the Jewish religion, women are just as important human beings as men are. The Bible states this fundamental idea very clearly, in telling the story of God's creation of all life. "Male and female created he them." The same act of creation applied to both man and woman, making them equal from the very beginning. Both were created in the image of God. That is to say, though God first created man, and then took a rib from Adam's side to create Eve, He created both Adam and Eve in the same spirit. Women have as much of the divine spirit in them as men have.

JEWISH TRADITION
Albert Einstein

The pursuit of knowledge for its own sake, an almost fanatical love of justice and the desire for personal independence — these are the features of Jewish tradition which make me thank my stars that I belong to it.

PHOTOGRAPHS: Title Page: *Sabbath Candelabrum,* brass, cast. Eastern Europe, 19th century. Hebrew inscription: "To kindle the Sabbath lights." Collection, The Jewish Museum, New York. Page 8: *Marriage Contract,* painting on parchment with cut work. Trieste, Italy, 1775. Gift of Dr. Harry G. Friedman. Collection, The Jewish Museum, New York. Page 16: *Torah Case and Torah for Sephardic Community,* case: silver, partly gilt, repousse, embossed, pressed and cast work. Paris, France, ca. 1860 by Maurice Mayer. Scroll: written on leather. Near Eastern. Collection, The Jewish Museum, New York. Page 36: *Torah Ark Curtain,* gold and silver applique and embroidery on violet silk. Height 85", Width 55". Italy, 1681. Gift of Dr. Harry G. Friedman, Collection, The Jewish Museum, New York. Pages 12, 20, 24, 28, 40, 44: Reed Holmes. Page 32: Myron Wang.

Set in Perpetua, a classic roman typeface
designed by Eric Gill in 1922.
Printed on Hallmark Crown Royale Book paper.
Designed by William Hunt.